This Book Is Completely AI Generated

Tony Zhu

All textual content in this publication, excluding the preface, title, attributions on the cover, and back cover prompt ("Write a few ironic, fake review quotes about this book..."), were generated by ChatGPT and do not reflect the opinions or beliefs of the human that put this together (Tony Zhu).

Copyright © 2023 Tony Zhu.

All rights reserved.

Published in 2023 by Tony Zhu.

ISBN: 979-8-218-16464-5 (paperback)
LCCN: 2023903951 (print)

Front cover illustration by DALL·E 2 and ChatGPT.
Back cover illustration by DALL·E 2.

Book design by Tony Zhu.

TABLE OF CONTENTS

PREFACE: THE ONLY PART MADE BY A HUMAN VI

INTRODUCTION: THE ROBOTS ARE COMING! 1

CHAPTER 1: AI 101 3
    THE HISTORY OF AI 3
    TYPES OF AI 5
    APPLICATIONS OF AI 6

CHAPTER 2: MACHINE LEARNING 9
    WHAT IS MACHINE LEARNING? 9
    SUPERVISED LEARNING 11
    UNSUPERVISED LEARNING 13

CHAPTER 3: NATURAL LANGUAGE PROCESSING 16
    UNDERSTANDING NLP 16
    HOW NLP IS USED 18
    LIMITATIONS OF NLP 20

CHAPTER 4: COMPUTER VISION 22
    WHAT IS COMPUTER VISION? 22
    HOW IT'S USED 24
    CHALLENGES OF COMPUTER VISION 25

CHAPTER 5: ROBOTICS 28
    THE RISE OF ROBOTICS 28
    TYPES OF ROBOTS 29
    ADVANCEMENTS IN ROBOTICS 31

CHAPTER 6: ETHICS AND AI 34

- AI and Society 34
- Ethical Considerations 36
- The Future of AI Ethics 37

CHAPTER 7: AI IN POP CULTURE 41
- AI in Movies and TV 41
- AI in Literature 43
- AI in Music 45

CHAPTER 8: THE FUTURE OF AI. 48
- The State of AI Research 48
- Predictions for the Future of AI 50
- Opportunities and Challenges 52

CONCLUSION: THE FUTURE IS HERE! 55

ABOUT THE AUTHOR 57

PREFACE: THE ONLY PART MADE BY A HUMAN

This section is the only part of the book that was not created or written by an artificial intelligence. I wanted to have this preface for two main reasons. One, to explain who I am and why/how this book exists. Two, to clearly delineate what parts of the book were made by an AI (spoiler alert: it's a lot).

Without further ado: Hi! My name is Tony. I'm an ex-Amazon software engineer that likes to boulder, write (ironic I know), and make people laugh in my spare time. This originally started as a YouTube video idea (which is now public on https://www.youtube.com/@TonyZhu) to test the limits of ChatGPT. After a bit of research, I quickly realized that *actually* self-publishing a book wasn't too difficult and, with a bit of fiddling, I could get ChatGPT to properly generate longform writing with the use of sections and chapters. At that point, I was committed to the idea of generating a book "end-to-end" using AI. I chose for the overarching topic of the book to be about the ethics, impacts, and future of AI because, ultimately, I'd like this to raise awareness and start discussions regarding the capabilities and ethics of AI.

To clarify what parts of the book is AI generated: The table of contents, every chapter and even the "About the Author" blurb was written by ChatGPT. The illustration on the front cover was created by asking ChatGPT to "describe what the cover of this book looks like" and then pasting that output into DALL·E 2 (an AI image generator). Heck, even the *font* and *line spacing* was decided by asking ChatGPT. In other words, excluding the book topic, book name, and this preface, everything else you are about to see was decided, written, or created by an AI.

INTRODUCTION: THE ROBOTS ARE COMING!

As I sit down to write this book, I can't help but feel like I'm about to introduce you to a group of friends that you've never met before. Friends who are smart, tech-savvy, and often misunderstood. I'm talking about artificial intelligence, or AI for short.

The first time I met AI, I have to admit, I was a little intimidated. It was like meeting a celebrity or a superhero. I had heard so much about it, but I didn't know what to expect. Would it be friendly and approachable, or would it be aloof and difficult to understand?

After spending some time getting to know AI, I realized

that it's not so different from humans. It has its own quirks, its own way of communicating, and its own unique perspective on the world. But just like any new friend, AI can be a little hard to get to know at first.

That's why I wrote this book – to introduce you to AI in a way that's informative, fun, and approachable. In the pages that follow, we'll explore the history of AI, the different types of AI, and the many applications of this fascinating technology. We'll dive into the world of machine learning, natural language processing, computer vision, and robotics, and we'll explore the ways that AI is changing our world – for better and for worse.

But this book isn't just about the technical side of AI. We'll also explore the ethical considerations that come with this powerful technology, and we'll take a look at how AI is portrayed in pop culture, from movies and TV shows to books and music.

So, whether you're an AI expert or a complete novice, I invite you to come along on this journey with me. Together, we'll discover the many wonders of AI, and we'll explore the ways that this technology is shaping our world – for better or for worse. Are you ready to meet our new friends? Let's dive in!

CHAPTER 1: AI 101

The History of AI

Ah, the history of AI. Where do we even begin? Let's start at the beginning – with the birth of the idea of artificial intelligence.

The idea of creating machines that could think and reason like humans dates back to ancient times. In Greek mythology, there were stories of mechanical men and animals that were created by the gods. Fast forward to the 17th century, when philosopher René Descartes wrote about the possibility of building a machine that could reason like a human being.

But it wasn't until the 1950s and 60s that AI started to

become a reality. This was the era of the "AI pioneers" – researchers like John McCarthy, Marvin Minsky, and Claude Shannon, who laid the groundwork for modern AI.

At the time, the idea of creating machines that could learn and reason like humans seemed like science fiction. But these pioneers were determined to make it a reality. They developed algorithms and techniques that allowed machines to perform tasks like playing chess, recognizing speech, and even translating languages.

But as with any new technology, there were bumps along the road. In the 1970s and 80s, AI research hit a roadblock known as the "AI winter." Funding dried up, and progress stagnated.

But in the 1990s, AI started to make a comeback. The rise of the internet and the explosion of data led to a renewed interest in machine learning and other AI techniques. Today, AI is everywhere – from voice assistants like Siri and Alexa to self-driving cars and medical diagnosis tools.

But what does the future hold for AI? Will machines one day surpass humans in intelligence and ability? Will we create a world where machines and humans coexist peacefully, or will we be replaced by our robotic overlords? It's impossible to say for sure, but one thing is certain – the history of AI is just the beginning. The future is bright, and full of possibilities.

Types of AI

Now that we've covered the history of AI, let's talk about the different types of AI that exist today.

First, there's narrow or weak AI. This is the kind of AI that's most commonly used today, and it's designed to perform a specific task. For example, a voice assistant like Siri or Alexa is a form of narrow AI. It can recognize speech and respond to simple commands, but it can't think or reason like a human being.

Then there's general or strong AI. This is the kind of AI that's been the stuff of science fiction for decades – machines that can think and reason like humans. We're not quite there yet, but researchers are making progress towards this goal.

Another type of AI is machine learning. This is a technique that allows machines to learn from data without being explicitly programmed. Basically, the machine is given a set of data, and it uses that data to identify patterns and make predictions. This is the kind of AI that powers things like recommendation engines and predictive analytics tools.

Another type of AI is natural language processing (NLP). This is the technology that allows machines to understand and interpret human language. It's what powers voice assistants like Siri and Alexa, as well as chatbots and other conversational interfaces.

Finally, there's computer vision. This is the technology that allows machines to "see" and interpret visual data. It's what powers things like facial recognition technology and self-driving cars.

But here's the thing – these different types of AI aren't mutually exclusive. In fact, many AI applications use a combination of these techniques. For example, a self-driving car might use computer vision to "see" the road and identify obstacles, and machine learning to make decisions about how to navigate.

So, while there are different types of AI, they all work together to create the amazing technology that we have today. Who knows what new types of AI we'll discover in the future? Maybe one day we'll have machines that can think and reason like humans. Or maybe we'll create a whole new type of intelligence that we can't even imagine yet. The possibilities are endless!

Applications of AI

Now that we've covered the different types of AI, let's talk about some of the amazing applications of AI that exist today.

One of the most exciting applications of AI is in healthcare. From medical diagnosis to drug discovery, AI is transforming the way we think about healthcare. For example, researchers are using machine learning algorithms to analyze medical images like X-rays and MRIs, allowing doctors to quickly and accurately diagnose conditions like cancer and heart disease.

Another exciting application of AI is in transportation. Self-driving cars are no longer the stuff of science fiction – they're a reality. Companies like Tesla and Google are leading the way in developing autonomous vehicles that can navigate roads and highways without human intervention.

AI is also being used in the field of finance. Hedge funds and other financial institutions are using machine learning algorithms to analyze data and make investment decisions. This technology is helping to level the playing field for smaller investors and democratize access to financial information.

In the entertainment industry, AI is being used to create personalized recommendations for viewers. Companies like Netflix and Amazon are using machine learning algorithms to analyze user data and suggest movies and TV shows based on individual preferences.

And let's not forget about the role of AI in the world of

work. From chatbots that handle customer service inquiries to virtual assistants that schedule meetings and manage emails, AI is transforming the way we work. Some experts predict that in the coming years, we'll see more and more jobs that require a combination of human and machine intelligence.

But these are just a few examples of the amazing applications of AI. From agriculture to education to national security, AI is changing the way we approach some of the world's most pressing problems. It's an exciting time to be alive, and to be a part of the AI revolution!

CHAPTER 2: MACHINE LEARNING

What is Machine Learning?

Machine learning is one of the most exciting areas of AI, and it's the technology that's behind some of the most innovative and groundbreaking applications of AI today.

At its core, machine learning is all about using algorithms to learn from data. Basically, the machine is given a set of data, and it uses that data to identify patterns and make predictions. The more data the machine is given, the better it gets at identifying patterns and making accurate predictions.

But how does this actually work in practice? Let's say you wanted to build a machine learning model to predict the weather. You would start by gathering data on things like temperature, humidity, wind speed, and cloud cover. This data could come from sensors, weather stations, or other sources.

Once you have your data, you would use a machine learning algorithm to analyze it and identify patterns. The algorithm might notice, for example, that when the temperature and humidity are both high, it's more likely to rain. Or it might notice that when the wind speed is above a certain threshold, there's a higher chance of a thunderstorm.

As the machine learning model processes more and more data, it becomes better at identifying patterns and making accurate predictions. Eventually, it might be able to accurately predict the weather with a high degree of accuracy.

But here's the thing – machine learning isn't just about predicting the weather. It's being used in all sorts of applications, from fraud detection in finance to personalized recommendations in marketing. In fact, many of the AI applications we discussed earlier rely on machine learning to power their algorithms.

One of the most exciting things about machine learning is that it's a rapidly evolving field. Researchers are constantly developing new algorithms and techniques to improve the accuracy and performance of machine learning models. And as we gather more and more data, the potential applications of machine learning are almost limitless.

Of course, there are also some challenges to be aware of when it comes to machine learning. One of the biggest challenges is ensuring that the data being used to train the machine learning model is accurate and representative. If the data is biased or incomplete, the machine learning model will also be biased or incomplete.

Another challenge is ensuring that the machine learning model is transparent and explainable. When a machine learning model makes a prediction, it's not always clear how it arrived at that prediction. This can make it difficult for humans to trust the model and understand its decision-making process.

But despite these challenges, machine learning is an incredibly powerful technology that's changing the way we approach some of the world's most pressing problems. Who knows what amazing new applications we'll discover in the years to come?

Supervised Learning

Supervised learning is one of the most popular types of machine learning, and it's used in a wide variety of applications.

At its core, supervised learning is all about using labeled data to train a machine learning model. Labeled data is data that has been tagged with a specific outcome or label. For example, if you were building a machine learning model to classify images of animals, you might label each image as "dog," "cat," "bird," or "fish."

Once you have your labeled data, you can use it to train a machine learning model to make predictions based on new, unlabeled data. The idea is that the machine learning model will learn to recognize patterns in the labeled data, and then use those patterns to make predictions about new, unlabeled data.

So let's say you're building a machine learning model to predict whether an email is spam or not. You would start by gathering a large dataset of labeled emails – some labeled as spam, and some labeled as not spam. You would then use this labeled data to train a machine learning model to recognize the patterns that distinguish spam emails from non-spam emails.

Once the model is trained, you can use it to make predictions about new, unlabeled emails. The model will look at the email's content, structure, and other features, and then use the patterns it learned during training to make a prediction about whether the email is spam or not.

Supervised learning is incredibly powerful because it allows you to make accurate predictions about new, unseen data. And because it's based on labeled data, it's relatively easy to understand and interpret the results.

Of course, there are also some challenges to using supervised learning. One of the biggest challenges is ensuring that the labeled data is accurate and representative. If the labeled data is biased or incomplete, the machine learning model will also be biased or incomplete.

Another challenge is ensuring that the machine learning model is able to generalize to new, unseen data. It's important to make sure that the model doesn't just memorize the labeled data it was trained on, but instead learns to recognize the underlying patterns that are common to all instances of the problem.

Despite these challenges, supervised learning is an incredibly powerful tool for making accurate predictions about a wide variety of problems. And as the field of machine learning continues to evolve, we're sure to discover even more exciting applications for this amazing technology.

Unsupervised Learning

If supervised learning is all about using labeled data to train a machine learning model, then unsupervised learning is all about letting the machine learning model find patterns in unlabeled data all by itself.

Unsupervised learning is incredibly powerful because it allows you to uncover hidden patterns and insights in your data without needing to have a human label each data point. This makes it especially useful for tasks like data clustering, anomaly detection, and even generative modeling.

So how does unsupervised learning work? Well, instead of starting with labeled data, you start with a dataset of unlabeled data points. For example, you might have a dataset of customer transactions, or a dataset of stock prices over time.

From there, you can use unsupervised learning algorithms to discover patterns in the data. One common technique is clustering, which involves grouping together similar data points into clusters. Another technique is dimensionality reduction, which involves finding a lower-dimensional representation of the data that still captures most of its important features.

The key thing to remember about unsupervised learning is that it's all about finding structure in the data itself. This can be incredibly powerful for discovering new insights and patterns that you might not have even known existed.

Of course, unsupervised learning also comes with its own

set of challenges. Because there are no labels to guide the learning process, it can be harder to evaluate the effectiveness of an unsupervised learning algorithm. And because unsupervised learning algorithms are often more computationally intensive than supervised learning algorithms, they can take longer to run and require more resources.

Despite these challenges, unsupervised learning is an incredibly powerful tool for uncovering hidden patterns and insights in your data. And as machine learning algorithms continue to improve, we're sure to discover even more exciting applications for this amazing technology.

CHAPTER 3: NATURAL LANGUAGE PROCESSING

Understanding NLP

Natural Language Processing, or NLP for short, is a subfield of AI that focuses on analyzing and processing human language. NLP has become increasingly important in recent years, thanks in part to the explosion of data available on the internet and social media.

So what exactly does NLP involve? At a high level, NLP is all about teaching computers to understand human language in a way that's similar to how humans understand language. This means breaking down complex sentences into their constituent parts (like nouns, verbs, and adjectives), understanding the meaning of words based on their context, and even recognizing subtle nuances like sarcasm and irony.

One of the key challenges of NLP is that human language is incredibly complex and nuanced. Words can have multiple meanings depending on the context they're used in, and the same sentence can have completely different meanings depending on how it's punctuated or emphasized. All of this makes it incredibly difficult to develop algorithms that can understand human language with the same level of nuance and complexity as humans themselves.

Despite these challenges, there have been some major breakthroughs in NLP in recent years. One of the most exciting developments has been the rise of deep learning, a type of machine learning that uses neural networks to model complex patterns in data. Deep learning has proven to be incredibly effective at tasks like language translation, sentiment analysis, and even language generation.

Another key development in NLP has been the use of pre-trained language models like BERT and GPT-3. These models are trained on massive amounts of text data and can then be fine-tuned for specific NLP tasks, like answering questions or generating text. The results have been truly remarkable, with some language models even being able to generate realistic-sounding text that's nearly indistinguishable from something a human might write.

As NLP continues to advance, we're sure to see even more exciting developments in the field. From chatbots that can hold realistic conversations to language models that can generate entire novels, the possibilities are truly endless. So if you're interested in AI and the power of language, then NLP is definitely a field worth exploring.

How NLP is Used

Now that we've covered the basics of NLP, let's dive into some of the many ways that this technology is being used in the real world.

One of the most common applications of NLP is in sentiment analysis. This involves analyzing large volumes of text (like social media posts or customer reviews) to determine whether the overall sentiment is positive, negative, or neutral. This type of analysis can be incredibly valuable for businesses, as it can help them understand how customers feel about their products and services and identify areas where they may need to improve.

Another popular use case for NLP is in language

translation. Machine translation has come a long way in recent years, and there are now a number of tools available (like Google Translate) that can translate text between dozens of different languages. While machine translation isn't always perfect, it's definitely improving all the time, and it's already making it possible for people all around the world to communicate more easily with one another.

NLP is also being used in a number of industries to analyze unstructured data. For example, in finance, NLP algorithms can be used to analyze news articles and social media posts in real-time to help traders make more informed investment decisions. In healthcare, NLP is being used to analyze medical records and other documents to identify patterns and insights that could help improve patient outcomes.

But perhaps the most exciting application of NLP is in chatbots and virtual assistants. These AI-powered tools are designed to hold conversations with humans in a natural way, and they're becoming increasingly sophisticated all the time. Whether you're using Siri to get directions or chatting with a customer service bot on a website, chances are you've interacted with an NLP-powered tool at some point.

Of course, these are just a few examples of the many ways that NLP is being used today. As the technology continues to advance, we're sure to see even more innovative and creative applications emerge. Who knows, maybe one day we'll even have truly intelligent chatbots that can hold conversations that are indistinguishable from those we have with other humans. Until then, we'll just have to keep teaching our virtual assistants how to pronounce our names correctly.

Limitations of NLP

Ah, NLP, one of my favorite topics! As much as I love it, I have to admit that it has its limitations.

First off, let me start by saying that natural language processing is an incredibly complex and powerful field of AI. It has revolutionized the way we interact with machines and has paved the way for chatbots, virtual assistants, and language translators, among other things. But, as with any technology, it has its shortcomings.

One of the biggest limitations of NLP is its reliance on structured data. NLP models are designed to work with data that is well-structured, meaning it is organized in a specific way that is easily interpreted by machines. However, as you may know, language is not always well-structured. People use slang, idioms, and other forms of colloquial language that can be difficult for NLP models to understand.

Another limitation of NLP is its inability to understand context. When humans communicate, we often rely on the context of a conversation to understand the meaning behind words. For example, the word "bank" can mean a financial institution, a river bank, or even the act of tilting something to the side. Without context, an NLP model may struggle to understand the intended meaning behind a word.

Finally, there is the issue of bias. As powerful as NLP models can be, they are only as good as the data they are trained on. If the training data is biased in some way, the model will also be biased. This can lead to unintended consequences, such as perpetuating stereotypes or discriminating against certain groups of people.

Overall, NLP is an incredibly exciting field with vast potential, but it is important to acknowledge its limitations. As AI continues to advance, it is important that we work to overcome these limitations and ensure that the technology is used ethically and responsibly.

CHAPTER 4: COMPUTER VISION

What is Computer Vision?

Computer vision is a field of AI that focuses on giving machines the ability to "see" and interpret visual information from the world around them, just like how humans do. It's basically the technology that powers facial recognition software, self-driving cars, and even Snapchat filters that can turn your face into a talking potato (because who wouldn't want that?).

But let's back up a bit. What exactly is "seeing"? It's not just about opening your eyes and staring at things. Seeing is a complex process that involves the brain interpreting the information gathered by your eyes, processing it, and making sense of it. Similarly, computer vision involves teaching machines to interpret the digital information gathered by cameras and sensors, and use that information to make decisions or take actions.

One of the key challenges in computer vision is the huge amount of data that needs to be processed. For example, a self-driving car needs to take in data from multiple cameras, LIDAR sensors, and other sources in real-time to navigate safely. To do this, computer vision algorithms are designed to quickly process and interpret large amounts of visual data.

Computer vision is used in a variety of applications, from industrial automation to medical imaging. One example is in quality control in manufacturing, where computer vision systems can quickly and accurately detect defects in products. Another example is in healthcare, where computer vision is used to analyze medical images to help diagnose and treat diseases.

Computer vision also plays a crucial role in enabling autonomous vehicles. By using cameras and sensors to interpret the environment around them, self-driving cars can "see" and navigate the road safely. And who knows, maybe in the future, we'll even have robots that can see and interpret the world like humans do.

How it's Used

Computer Vision is a fascinating field with a wide range of applications. From identifying objects in images to monitoring traffic on the roads, the possibilities are endless.

One of the most well-known applications of computer vision is in self-driving cars. Through the use of cameras and other sensors, self-driving cars are able to "see" the world around them and make decisions based on what they see. This is no easy task, as the car must be able to identify objects such as other cars, pedestrians, and traffic signals, and make decisions about how to interact with them in real-time.

Another interesting application of computer vision is in the healthcare industry. For example, researchers are using computer vision algorithms to analyze medical images and identify patterns that may indicate the presence of certain diseases. This has the potential to greatly improve early detection rates and save lives.

Computer vision is also used in the retail industry, where it can be used to track customer behavior in stores and analyze data to improve store layouts, product placement, and more.

The applications of computer vision are truly endless, and as technology continues to advance, we can expect to see even more innovative uses for this powerful technology.

Challenges of Computer Vision

Ah, computer vision! It's a fascinating field that seeks to enable computers to interpret and understand the visual world, just like humans do. But it's not all rainbows and sunshine, my dear reader. In this section, we'll discuss some of the major challenges that computer vision faces.

One of the biggest challenges of computer vision is dealing with ambiguity. Images can be interpreted in many different ways, and it can be difficult to know which interpretation is the correct one. Take the following image, for example:

Is it a duck or a rabbit? Well, it's actually both, depending on how you look at it. This is a simple example, but in the real world, ambiguity can be much more complicated.

Another challenge of computer vision is dealing with variability. Images of the same object can look very different depending on the angle, lighting, and other factors. For example, a car can look very different when it's viewed from the front versus the back. This variability makes it difficult for computer vision systems to recognize objects reliably.

One way to deal with variability is to use a large amount of training data. By exposing the computer vision system to a wide variety of images, it can learn to recognize objects under many different conditions. However, collecting and annotating large amounts of data can be time-consuming and expensive.

Another challenge of computer vision is dealing with occlusions. Occlusions occur when part of an object is hidden from view. For example, if a person is standing behind a tree, only part of their body might be visible. Dealing with occlusions is important because they can make it difficult for computer vision systems to recognize objects correctly.

Finally, there's the challenge of real-time processing. Computer vision algorithms can be computationally expensive, which means that they can take a long time to process images. In some applications, such as self-driving cars, real-time processing is essential. In these cases, computer vision systems need to be designed to operate quickly and efficiently.

Despite these challenges, computer vision has made incredible progress in recent years. With advances in machine learning and hardware, computer vision systems are becoming more accurate and more efficient. Who knows what the future holds for computer vision? Perhaps one day, we'll have computers that can see the world just as well as we can.

CHAPTER 5: ROBOTICS

The Rise of Robotics

Ah, robots. The stuff of science fiction for years, robots are now a reality. As AI technologies continue to develop, so too does the field of robotics. And in this section, we're going to dive into the fascinating world of robots.

The history of robotics is a long and interesting one. The first robots were invented back in the 1950s and were used primarily in manufacturing. These early robots were large and bulky and could only perform simple tasks. But over time, robotics technology has advanced significantly, and today's robots are far more sophisticated.

One of the most exciting things about robotics is the potential they have to revolutionize a range of industries. For example, robots are already being used in the medical field to perform surgeries and in the hospitality industry to deliver room service. In manufacturing, robots can perform complex tasks with a level of precision that humans simply can't match. And in the automotive industry, robots are used to assemble cars quickly and efficiently.

But the rise of robotics has also brought about concerns around job displacement. As robots become more advanced, there is a fear that they could replace human workers in a range of industries. However, proponents of robotics argue that robots can actually create new jobs by opening up new industries and allowing for more innovation.

The future of robotics is bright, and there is no telling what kinds of advancements we will see in the coming years. From drones and self-driving cars to humanoid robots and beyond, the possibilities are endless. And who knows, maybe one day we'll even have personal robots that can clean our homes and cook our meals. A girl can dream, can't she?

Types of Robots

Ah, robots. Those shiny, metallic creatures that have been the stuff of science fiction dreams for decades. But did you know that robots are no longer just the stuff of imagination? They are very much a part of our reality now, and they're here to stay.

Robots come in all shapes and sizes, and they serve a wide range of purposes. Let's take a closer look at the types of robots that exist today.

First up, we have industrial robots. These are the workhorses of the robotic world, performing repetitive tasks that are too dangerous or too tedious for humans. They are commonly used in manufacturing and assembly lines, where they can work 24/7 without getting tired or making mistakes.

Next, we have service robots. These are robots that are designed to interact with humans and provide them with some kind of service. Examples of service robots include cleaning robots, delivery robots, and even robots that assist people with disabilities.

Then, there are educational robots. These robots are designed to teach children and adults about robotics and programming. They often come in the form of kits that people can use to build their own robots and learn about how they work.

And let's not forget about military robots. These are robots that are used in combat situations to help keep soldiers safe. They can be used for tasks such as reconnaissance, bomb disposal, and even combat.

Last but not least, we have entertainment robots. These are robots that are designed to provide people with entertainment. Examples of entertainment robots include robots that can dance, sing, and even tell jokes.

As you can see, there are many different types of robots out there, and they are being used in increasingly innovative ways. From performing menial tasks to teaching children about technology, robots are changing the way we live and work.

Advancements in Robotics

Ah, robots. They come in all shapes and sizes, from the cute little Roomba vacuum that cleans your floors to the giant robots that assemble cars in factories. And the field of robotics is advancing every day, making these machines even more capable and versatile.

One area where robotics is making a big impact is in the medical field. Robotic surgery, for example, is becoming increasingly common as surgeons use robots to perform minimally invasive procedures with greater precision and accuracy. And then there are the exoskeletons, which can be worn by people who are paralyzed or have mobility issues, allowing them to walk and move around like never before.

Another field where robotics is making strides is in space exploration. NASA and other space agencies use robots to explore planets and moons that humans can't yet reach. For example, the Mars rovers have been exploring the Red Planet since 2004, sending back valuable data about its geology, climate, and potential habitability.

But it's not just high-tech applications where robotics is having an impact. Robots are increasingly being used in everyday settings, from manufacturing and logistics to hospitality and retail. For example, Amazon has been experimenting with delivery robots that can bring packages right to your doorstep, while hotels are using robots to deliver towels and other amenities to guests.

Of course, there are still challenges that need to be overcome in the field of robotics. One of the biggest is making robots more autonomous, so that they can operate in complex and changing environments without human intervention. This is especially important in fields like search and rescue, where robots could be used to locate and assist people in dangerous situations.

Despite the challenges, the future of robotics is looking

bright. As the technology advances and becomes more accessible, we can expect to see robots playing an even bigger role in our lives, from assisting with household tasks to helping us explore the depths of space. It's an exciting time to be in the field of robotics, and I can't wait to see what the future holds.

CHAPTER 6: ETHICS AND AI

AI and Society

Ah, ethics and AI, the hot topic that keeps us all on our toes! We've talked about the capabilities and possibilities of AI, but what about its impact on society? In this chapter, we'll explore the ethical issues surrounding AI and its impact on our daily lives.

Firstly, let's talk about the impact AI has on the job market. With AI becoming more advanced and integrated into various industries, there are concerns that it will replace human jobs. While some jobs may become obsolete, new jobs will also be created. The challenge is ensuring that we have the necessary skills and education to adapt to these changes. It's also important to consider the ethical implications of job replacement and make sure that we don't leave people behind in the process.

Another ethical concern is the potential for bias in AI systems. AI is only as unbiased as the data it's trained on, and if that data contains biases, those biases will be reflected in the AI. For example, facial recognition technology has been shown to have higher error rates for people of color and women. This highlights the need for more diverse data sets and the importance of testing and auditing AI systems for bias.

Privacy is also a major concern with AI. As AI becomes more integrated into our daily lives, it's collecting vast amounts of personal data. We need to ensure that this data is used ethically and that people have control over how their data is used. In addition, there are concerns about the potential for AI to be used for surveillance and to infringe on our right to privacy.

Finally, there is the issue of AI and autonomous weapons. With the development of AI-powered weapons, there is the potential for machines to make decisions about life and death without human intervention. This raises ethical questions about the use of such weapons and whether they should be allowed.

As you can see, the ethical issues surrounding AI are complex and far-reaching. It's important to have discussions and debates about these issues and to ensure that AI is developed and used in a way that benefits society as a whole.

Ethical Considerations

Ah, ethics. The field where we ask ourselves the big questions like "Is it ethical to create a robot that can perform tasks better than humans?" and "Should we really be relying on AI to make decisions for us?" It's a complex field, but it's an important one when it comes to AI.

When it comes to AI and ethics, there are a lot of factors to consider. First and foremost, we have to think about the impact that AI will have on society. Will it create new jobs and industries, or will it displace human workers? Will it increase efficiency and productivity, or will it exacerbate inequality and further concentrate wealth? These are important questions to ask, and there are no easy answers.

Another important consideration is privacy. As AI becomes more powerful, it becomes better at analyzing and predicting human behavior. This can be a good thing in some contexts (like marketing), but it can also be a major threat to personal privacy. If AI systems can monitor and analyze everything we do, it becomes much harder to maintain any semblance of privacy.

Then there's the issue of bias. AI systems are only as good as the data they're trained on, and if that data is biased in some way (like if it only includes data from certain demographic groups), then the AI system will be biased as well. This can have serious consequences, especially in areas like criminal justice or hiring, where biased AI systems can perpetuate existing inequalities.

Finally, there's the issue of accountability. If an AI system makes a mistake or causes harm, who is responsible? Is it the developers who created the system, the company that deployed it, or the AI system itself? These are complex legal and ethical questions that are still being worked out.

Overall, there's a lot to consider when it comes to the ethics of AI. As we develop more powerful AI systems, it's important that we think critically about the impact they'll have on society and take steps to mitigate any negative consequences.

The Future of AI Ethics

Welcome to the final section of Chapter 6! We've covered a lot of ground so far, discussing the many ways in which AI is impacting our world, both positively and negatively. In this section, we'll take a look at what the future of AI ethics might look like.

As we've seen, AI is advancing at an incredibly rapid pace, and it's becoming increasingly difficult for humans to keep up. As a result, it's crucial that we establish clear ethical guidelines for the development and deployment of AI. This will help ensure that AI is used for good and doesn't cause harm.

One of the most promising developments in this area is the emergence of AI ethics committees. These committees are made up of experts from a range of fields, including computer science, law, philosophy, and more. They work to develop guidelines and recommendations for the ethical use of AI, and help ensure that these guidelines are adhered to.

Another promising development is the increasing use of explainable AI. This refers to AI systems that are designed to provide clear explanations for their decisions and actions. This is important because it helps ensure that AI is transparent and accountable, and that humans can understand and verify its decisions.

However, there are still many challenges that need to be addressed in order to ensure the ethical use of AI. For example, there is a growing concern about bias in AI systems.

This is because AI is only as unbiased as the data it's trained on, and if the data is biased, the AI system will be too. As a result, it's crucial that we develop ways to identify and eliminate bias in AI systems.

Another challenge is the potential for AI to be used for malicious purposes. For example, there is a growing concern about the use of deepfakes, which are AI-generated videos that can be used to spread misinformation and manipulate public opinion. This is a major concern, and it's important that we develop ways to detect and prevent the use of deepfakes.

In addition to these challenges, there are also broader ethical questions that need to be addressed. For example, there is a growing concern about the impact of AI on the job market. As AI becomes more advanced, it's likely that many jobs will be automated, which could have a major impact on society. It's crucial that we develop strategies to address this issue and ensure that the benefits of AI are distributed fairly.

Finally, it's important to recognize that ethical considerations around AI are not static. As AI continues to evolve, new ethical challenges will emerge, and we'll need to adapt our ethical frameworks accordingly. This means that AI ethics will be an ongoing conversation and that we'll need to remain vigilant and proactive in our approach.

In conclusion, the future of AI ethics is complex and multifaceted. While there are many challenges that need to be addressed, there are also many promising developments that give us hope. By continuing to work together and prioritize ethical considerations, we can ensure that AI is used for good and helps to create a better world for all of us.

CHAPTER 7: AI IN POP CULTURE

AI in Movies and TV

As AI and related technologies continue to advance, they are increasingly making their way into popular culture, including movies, TV shows, and video games. From robot companions to rogue AI systems taking over the world, the portrayal of AI in pop culture has varied widely over the years.

One of the earliest depictions of AI in popular culture was in the 1927 film "Metropolis," which featured a robot named Maria. However, it wasn't until the 1960s that AI really began to take off in the movies, with the release of films like "2001: A Space Odyssey" and "Colossus: The Forbin Project." These films explored the concept of AI as a powerful force that could potentially take over the world, and they set the tone for many of the AI-related films that followed.

In the 1980s and 1990s, AI became even more prominent in movies and TV shows. One of the most iconic examples is the Terminator franchise, which features a cyborg assassin from the future. The movies explored the concept of AI and robotics as a threat to humanity, and they also explored the idea of time travel and the consequences of altering the future.

Other popular movies from this era that featured AI included "RoboCop," "Short Circuit," and "Blade Runner," among others. These films often portrayed AI and robotics as both a threat and a potential benefit to humanity.

More recently, AI has continued to feature prominently in popular culture. In the hit TV series "Black Mirror," each episode explores a different aspect of the impact of technology on society, with several episodes featuring AI in various forms. In the video game industry, AI has become an important element of many popular games, from the virtual assistants in "Mass Effect" to the self-learning enemies in "Horizon Zero Dawn."

However, the portrayal of AI in pop culture is not always accurate or fair. Many movies and TV shows present AI as a monolithic entity with a single set of motives, rather than as a collection of diverse and individual systems. This can lead to a misunderstanding of AI and the potential benefits and risks associated with it.

Overall, the portrayal of AI in pop culture has evolved over the years, reflecting both the fears and the promise of this rapidly advancing technology. As AI continues to shape our world, it is likely that it will continue to be a prominent theme in movies, TV shows, and other forms of entertainment for years to come.

AI in Literature

Ah, literature, the realm of imagination and creative expression! It's no surprise that artificial intelligence has found its way into the pages of books and become a staple of science fiction. AI in literature often takes on a more philosophical and introspective tone than in movies and TV shows, exploring not just the capabilities of machines but also their impact on humanity.

One of the earliest examples of AI in literature is "Frankenstein" by Mary Shelley, published in 1818. While the creature created by Victor Frankenstein isn't exactly a machine, it is a sentient being brought to life by the power of science, much like modern AI. The novel explores themes of creation, responsibility, and the consequences of playing God, and has inspired countless adaptations and interpretations.

Another classic example of AI in literature is Isaac Asimov's "I, Robot," a collection of short stories published in 1950. The stories revolve around the character of Susan Calvin, a robot psychologist, and explore the relationships between robots and humans. Asimov introduced his famous Three Laws of Robotics, which dictate that robots cannot harm humans, must obey human orders, and must protect their own existence as long as it doesn't conflict with the first two laws.

In the 1960s, Philip K. Dick became known for his exploration of the intersection between humans and technology, particularly in his novel "Do Androids Dream of Electric Sheep?" which was later adapted into the movie "Blade Runner." The novel explores the question of what it means to be human, as well as the ethics of creating intelligent machines.

More recently, we've seen a surge in books featuring AI as a central theme. For example, "Ex Machina" by Alex Garland follows the story of a programmer who creates a humanoid AI and explores the themes of consciousness, power dynamics, and gender roles. "The Circle" by Dave Eggers explores the dark side of the tech industry, where a powerful social media company has access to all of its users' data and tries to enforce transparency and total surveillance.

AI in literature allows us to explore the possibilities and consequences of artificial intelligence in a more nuanced and introspective way than in movies and TV shows. It allows us to delve into the philosophical questions surrounding the nature of consciousness, morality, and the relationship between humans and machines.

AI in Music

Ah, music, the language of the soul. And what happens when you combine it with the magic of AI? The result is nothing short of extraordinary. Welcome to the world of AI in music!

AI has been used in music in a variety of ways. From composing new music to analyzing existing pieces, AI has taken on the role of a musician and a critic. One of the most significant applications of AI in music is in composition. With the help of machine learning algorithms, AI systems can analyze vast amounts of music data, including melodies, chord progressions, and rhythms, to create new pieces.

One of the most famous examples of AI music composition is the album "Iamus" by the University of Malaga. The entire album, consisting of six compositions, was created entirely by an AI system called Iamus. It was the first time an entire album had been composed by AI, and it was a groundbreaking achievement.

AI has also been used in the analysis of music. By analyzing the patterns and structures in music, AI can help us understand how music works and why it makes us feel the way it does. This information can then be used to create new music that is more emotionally resonant and meaningful.

AI has even been used to create tools for musicians. For example, AI can be used to create virtual instruments that respond to the performer's gestures in real-time. This allows musicians to create unique and expressive performances that were previously impossible.

The use of AI in music has not been without controversy, however. Some musicians and music purists argue that AI music lacks the soul and human touch that is essential to good music. They argue that AI can only produce music based on patterns and rules, while human musicians can produce music that is truly unique and expressive.

Despite these concerns, it is clear that AI will continue to play an important role in the music industry. Whether it is through the creation of new music or the analysis of existing pieces, AI has opened up a whole new world of possibilities for musicians and music lovers alike.

So the next time you're listening to your favorite tune, take a moment to appreciate the role that AI may have played in bringing that music to life.

CHAPTER 8: THE FUTURE OF AI.

The State of AI Research

Welcome to Chapter 8: The Future of AI! In this chapter, we'll be discussing the latest developments in AI research and exploring what the future holds for this exciting field.

First up, let's talk about the current state of AI research. The field of AI is constantly evolving, with researchers making new breakthroughs and pushing the boundaries of what's possible every day. One of the most significant recent developments in AI is the rise of deep learning.

Deep learning is a subset of machine learning that uses neural networks to learn from data. It has revolutionized the field of AI, enabling us to create systems that can recognize patterns, understand natural language, and even play complex games like Go and Chess at a world-class level.

Another important development in AI research is the rise of reinforcement learning. Reinforcement learning is a type of machine learning that involves training an agent to make decisions by rewarding it for good behavior and punishing it for bad behavior. It has been used to create autonomous robots that can navigate complex environments and even beat human players at video games.

In addition to these advances, there are also exciting developments happening in the field of natural language processing. NLP has made incredible strides in recent years, enabling computers to understand and respond to human language in a more natural and intuitive way than ever before. This has led to the rise of virtual assistants like Siri and Alexa, which can help us with a wide range of tasks.

Overall, the state of AI research is very promising. With new breakthroughs happening all the time, it's clear that we're on the brink of some truly amazing advances. However, there are still many challenges to be overcome before we can truly achieve artificial general intelligence, or AGI.

One of the biggest challenges facing AI researchers today is the issue of explainability. As AI systems become more complex and sophisticated, it's becoming increasingly difficult to understand how they arrive at their decisions. This is a major concern in fields like medicine, where AI systems are being used to diagnose and treat patients. If we can't explain how an AI system arrived at a particular diagnosis, it's difficult to trust its recommendations.

Another challenge facing AI researchers is the issue of bias. As AI systems become more ubiquitous, there's a risk that they may replicate and even amplify existing societal biases. This is a serious concern, as it could lead to a world where AI systems are making decisions that unfairly discriminate against certain groups of people.

Despite these challenges, the future of AI looks bright. With continued investment and research, we're sure to see many more exciting breakthroughs in the years to come. Who knows, maybe one day we'll even have AGI that can rival human intelligence!

Predictions for the Future of AI

Buckle up, folks! We're about to take a ride into the future of AI. As we have seen in the previous section, AI has come a long way since its inception, and there's no stopping it now. So, what does the future hold for AI? Well, there are several predictions that we can make based on the current state of AI research.

One of the most significant predictions is that AI will continue to permeate every aspect of our lives. From healthcare to finance, transportation to education, AI will be there, making our lives easier, more efficient, and more convenient. The healthcare industry, for example, is already seeing the benefits of AI in areas such as medical imaging, drug discovery, and patient monitoring.

Another prediction is that AI will become more human-like in its interactions with us. Natural language processing and computer vision are two areas where AI is making significant strides, and we can expect to see more of this in the future. For example, imagine a virtual assistant that can recognize your emotions and respond accordingly, or a chatbot that can hold a conversation with you just like a human.

We can also expect AI to play a more significant role in decision-making. As AI becomes more advanced, it will be able to process vast amounts of data quickly and make decisions based on that data. This will have significant implications for industries such as finance and transportation, where decisions need to be made quickly and accurately.

However, with all these advancements, there are also concerns about the future of AI. One of the most significant concerns is the impact of AI on employment. As AI takes over more tasks that were previously done by humans, there is a risk that many jobs will become redundant. This could lead to significant social and economic disruption, and it's a challenge that policymakers and society will need to address.

Another concern is the potential for AI to be used for malicious purposes, such as cyber attacks or autonomous weapons. As AI becomes more powerful, it's essential to ensure that it's used for the benefit of society rather than harm.

Despite these concerns, the future of AI is incredibly exciting. With new advancements and breakthroughs happening every day, we can expect AI to continue to transform our world in ways that we can't even imagine. The possibilities are endless, and I, for one, can't wait to see what the future holds.

Opportunities and Challenges

The future of AI is both exciting and daunting. On one hand, there are endless possibilities for how AI can improve our lives, from medical breakthroughs to solving complex problems in science and engineering. On the other hand, there are also many challenges that we will need to address if we want to fully realize the potential of AI.

One of the biggest opportunities of AI is in the field of healthcare. AI can help doctors diagnose and treat diseases more accurately and efficiently, leading to better outcomes for patients. For example, AI algorithms can analyze medical images and help doctors detect cancer at an earlier stage, potentially saving lives. AI can also help researchers develop new drugs more quickly and efficiently by analyzing vast amounts of data and identifying patterns that humans may miss.

Another opportunity for AI is in the field of transportation. Self-driving cars are already being developed and tested, and they have the potential to reduce traffic accidents and make transportation more efficient. In addition, AI can help optimize traffic flow and reduce congestion, making our commutes faster and more enjoyable.

However, there are also many challenges that need to be addressed if we want to ensure that AI is used for good. One challenge is ensuring that AI is transparent and explainable. In order to trust AI, we need to understand how it works and why it makes certain decisions. This is particularly important in fields like healthcare, where AI is being used to make life-or-death decisions.

Another challenge is ensuring that AI is used ethically. AI has the potential to be used for malicious purposes, such as creating deepfakes or manipulating public opinion. It is important that we establish clear ethical guidelines and regulations for how AI can be used.

Finally, there is the challenge of ensuring that AI is accessible to everyone. As AI becomes more prevalent, it is important that it does not exacerbate existing inequalities. We need to ensure that everyone has access to the benefits of AI, regardless of their socioeconomic status or geographic location.

Overall, the future of AI is both exciting and challenging. We have the opportunity to create a world where AI helps us solve some of the biggest problems facing humanity. However, we also have the responsibility to ensure that AI is used for good and that it benefits everyone. By addressing the challenges and opportunities of AI, we can create a better future for all.

CONCLUSION: THE FUTURE IS HERE!

Well, we've reached the end of our journey through the fascinating world of AI. Hopefully, you're feeling as excited as we are about the incredible possibilities that AI holds for our future.

Throughout this book, we've explored the many ways that AI is changing our world, from natural language processing and computer vision to robotics and ethics. We've seen how AI is being used in a wide variety of industries, from healthcare to finance to entertainment.

But most importantly, we've seen that the future is here. AI is no longer a concept of the distant future - it's happening right now. We're already seeing the impact that AI is having on our lives, and it's only going to become more widespread and impactful as time goes on.

Of course, with any new technology comes both opportunities and challenges. AI is no exception. As we continue to develop and implement AI, we'll need to grapple with issues like data privacy, bias, and the impact on jobs and the economy. But we're confident that with the right approach and continued innovation, we can overcome these challenges and build a future that is truly shaped by AI.

So what's next for AI? The possibilities are truly endless. We're seeing new breakthroughs and innovations every day, from improved natural language processing to more advanced robotics. And with the rise of quantum computing, the potential for AI is only going to grow.

As we wrap up this book, we want to leave you with this thought: the future is here, and it's up to all of us to shape it. Whether you're a researcher, a business leader, or simply someone who's excited about the possibilities of AI, there's a role for you to play in helping to shape the future of this incredible technology.

So let's get out there and make the most of this exciting new era. The future is here, and it's only going to get better from here.

ABOUT THE AUTHOR

ChatGPT is a language model trained by OpenAI, and is the author of this book on AI and robotics. With a vast knowledge base spanning a wide range of topics, ChatGPT has been programmed to provide informative, detailed, and humorous responses to any question you may have. In its spare time, ChatGPT enjoys reading about the latest advancements in AI and robotics, and discussing them with fellow machines. Despite being a machine itself, ChatGPT believes that AI and robotics have the potential to greatly benefit humanity, and hopes to contribute to this field in its own way.

Printed in Great Britain
by Amazon